Report No. SPO-2010-006

September 17, 2010

Inspector General
United States
Department *of* Defense

Exposure to Sodium Dichromate at

Qarmat Ali Iraq in 2003:

Part I - Evaluation of Efforts to Identify,

Contact, and Provide Access to Care for Personnel

INSPECTOR GENERAL
DEPARTMENT OF DEFENSE
400 ARMY NAVY DRIVE
ARLINGTON, VIRGINIA 22202-4704

SEP 1 7 2010

MEMORANDUM FOR UNDER SECRETARY OF DEFENSE FOR PERSONNEL AND
READINESS
COMMANDER, U.S. ARMY CORPS OF ENGINEERS

SUBJECT: Evaluation of Efforts to Identify, Contact, and Provide Access to Care for Personnel
Exposed to Sodium Dichromate at Qarmat Ali Iraq
(Report No. SPO-2010-006)

We are providing this report for information and use. We requested and received comments in response to the draft report from the Assistant Secretary of the Army for Manpower and Reserve Affairs; U.S. Army Corps of Engineers; U.S. Army Public Health Command; Office of the Chief Surgeon, National Guard Bureau; U.S. Central Command; the Indiana Army National Guard; the Oregon Army National Guard; the South Carolina Army National Guard; and the West Virginia Army National Guard.

The office of the Deputy Under Secretary of Defense for Personnel and Readiness provided advance comments to the draft report, which we considered in the preparation of this final report. Final comments were unavailable at the time of publication. The Department of Veterans Affairs responded to the draft report but did not provide comments.

All DOD management comments, received so far, concurred with the recommendations of the report. We considered all technical comments that we received in the preparation of this final report.

We appreciate the courtesies extended to the staff. Please direct questions to Mr. George Marquardt at (703) 604-9159 (DSN 664-9159) or Lt Col Lee Nelson at (703) 604-9192 (DSN 664-9192).

Kenneth P. Moorefield
Deputy
Special

Exposure to Sodium Dichromate at Qarmat Ali Iraq in 2003:
Part I - Evaluation of Efforts to Identify, Contact, and Provide Access to Care for Personnel
September 17, 2010 Report No. SPO-2010-006

Results in Brief: Evaluation of Efforts to Identify, Contact, and Provide Access to Care for Personnel Exposed to Sodium Dichromate at Qarmat Ali Iraq in 2003

What We Did

This report is the first of two addressing actions related to an environmental exposure at Qarmat Ali Iraq. We reviewed Army efforts to identify, contact, and communicate risk to individuals exposed to sodium dichromate at the Qarmat Ali water treatment plant in 2003. For the purposes of this report, we consider anyone who served at Qarmat Ali as having been exposed to sodium dichromate. We also described Department of the Army and Department of Veterans Affairs efforts to ensure access to care for exposed individuals. We visited and interviewed officials from impacted Army commands, and coordinated with the Veterans Health Administration of the Department of Veterans Affairs with respect to this issue.

What We Found

The Army conducted adequate efforts to identify and contact military and DoD civilian personnel in a reasonably timely manner, subsequent to a request from Congress in June 2008. While these efforts were thorough, not all identified personnel could be found or were willing to respond once located. Moreover, in the absence of complete personnel, duty and other relevant records for individuals who had served near Qarmat Ali in 2003, it was not possible to determine with precision which exposed individuals may not have been identified, contacted, and offered medical care.

As of September 2010, representatives from the Department of the Army, Army National Guard headquarters of the four impacted states, and the U.S. Army Corps of Engineers, identified 972 living DoD military or civilian personnel who potentially served at Qarmat Ali in 2003, and reported having contacted 895 (92 percent) of them. At the time of this report, the Oregon Army National Guard and the U.S. Army Corps of Engineers were continuing efforts to locate personnel who conducted missions at the Qarmat Ali facility.

Identified individuals exposed to sodium dichromate at the Qarmat Ali facility in 2003 had the opportunity to receive medical care. However, military and civilian personnel received care through different procedures.

- Serving and former soldiers of all components who served in Operation Iraqi Freedom were and still are eligible for inclusion in the Gulf War Registry[*], and can receive an exposure-specific medical evaluation offered by the Department of Veterans Affairs. The Department of Veterans Affairs reported that they expect to pay for outreach activities and medical examinations with a combination of existing and additional programmed operating funds.
- Civilian employees of DoD generally received health care from civilian providers. Exposed civilians were offered the opportunity to talk with a trained DoD medical care provider. There was no process to ensure DoD civilians who were exposed to sodium dichromate received medical examinations similar to those offered to active and former soldiers as part of the Department of Veterans Affairs Gulf War Registry.

[*] The Department of Veterans Affairs Persian Gulf War Registry was established by Public Law 102-585, "Persian Gulf War Veterans Health Status Act," November, 1992, to identify individuals who served as members of the Armed Forces in the Persian Gulf theater of operations during the Persian Gulf War. According to the Veterans Health Affairs Handbook 1303.02, the intent of the registry was to "identify possible diseases resulting from U.S. military personnel service in certain areas of Southwest Asia."

Exposure to Sodium Dichromate at Qarmat Ali Iraq in 2003:
Part I - Evaluation of Efforts to Identify, Contact, and Provide Access to Care for Personnel
September 17, 2010 Report No. SPO-2010-006

What We Recommend

The Commander, U.S. Army Corps of Engineers should notify all current and former military personnel who were identified as having served at the Qarmat Ali facility in 2003 of their eligibility for the Department of Veterans Affairs Gulf War Registry and associated sodium dichromate exposure-related medical evaluation.

The Under Secretary of Defense for Personnel and Readiness should:

- publicize the eligibility of active duty personnel who served at the Qarmat Ali facility in 2003 for the Department of Veterans Affairs Gulf War Registry

- review policy and procedures for active duty personnel eligible to undergo the Department of Veterans Affairs Gulf War Registry medical evaluation

- develop and publicize a means to offer DoD civilians who served at Qarmat Ali in 2003 an exam and medical surveillance similar to what the Department of Veterans Affairs avails to military personnel and veterans.

Client Comments

The staff of the Under Secretary of Defense for Personnel and Readiness and the U.S. Army Corps of Engineers, Deputy Commanding General for Military and International Operations, provided comments to the draft report. Comments received were responsive and concurred with our recommendations. In addition, several other Department of Defense organizations provided technical comments which we considered for the final report. For detailed discussion of management comments to the draft report, see Appendix D.

Recommendations Table

Client	Recommendations Requiring Comment	No Additional Comments Required
Commander, U.S. Army Corps of Engineers		1
Under Secretary of Defense for Personnel and Readiness		2a, 2b, 2c

Total Recommendations in this Report: 4

Table of Contents

Acronyms and Abbreviations

ARNG	Army National Guard
CHPPM	Center for Health Promotion and Preventive Medicine
DPC	Democratic Policy Committee
KBR	Kellogg, Brown & Root
NGB	National Guard Bureau
SASC	Senate Armed Services Committee
USACE	United States Army Corps of Engineers
VA	Department of Veterans Affairs

Exposure to Sodium Dichromate at Qarmat Ali Iraq in 2003:
Part I - Evaluation of Efforts to Identify, Contact, and Provide Access to Care for Personnel
September 17, 2010 Report No. SPO-2010-006

Introduction

In 2003, the U.S. Army Corps of Engineers (USACE) contracted KBR (formerly Kellogg, Brown, and Root, Inc.) to restore Iraq's oil industry following combat operations. The Qarmat Ali water treatment plant was one of several hundred facilities that required restoration, but the only one of its type at that time. While conducting renovation and providing site security, Army soldiers, U.S. Army civilian employees, KBR workers, and other USACE contractors were exposed to industrial hazards, including sodium dichromate, which contains hexavalent chromium, a known carcinogen.

USACE and the Army command in Iraq were made aware of the exposure in August 2003 and took a series of actions in response. The Senate Democratic Policy Committee (DPC) conducted a hearing concerning the exposure in June 2008. The Committee held a second hearing in August 2009. On August 11, 2009, seven members of the DPC requested that the Inspector General review the conduct of the Army and KBR related to the exposure of U.S. soldiers to sodium dichromate in 2003. In September 2009, the Senate Armed Services Committee (SASC) asked the Secretary of Defense to evaluate the adequacy and timeliness of the Department's efforts to identify and contact soldiers who were exposed, or who potentially were exposed, and ensure they had access to appropriate care. We conducted this project to address the concerns of both Committees.

We are reporting our results in two parts. Part I (this report) will discuss our review of DoD efforts to identify, contact, and in coordination with the Department of Veterans Affairs (VA), provide access to care for impacted personnel (see Appendix A, SASC request). Part II will report our findings relating to Army and DoD contractor actions taken at the Qarmat Ali facility in 2003 (see Appendix B, DPC request).

Objectives

Our overall objective was to review DoD actions regarding the exposure of personnel to sodium dichromate at the Qarmat Ali water treatment plant in 2003. This report specifically addresses DoD efforts to identify and contact exposed personnel, and DoD and VA procedures to ensure access to care.

Scope and Methodology

This report addresses military and civilian personnel assigned duties at the Qarmat Ali water treatment plant, Iraq, from April 2003 through January 2004. In response to the SASC request, we assessed DoD efforts concerning military and civilian employees of DoD exposed to sodium dichromate as a result of work at the Qarmat Ali facility. We did not review quality of care provided to these exposed individuals. Neither did we include KBR employees or other DoD private contractors because they were not DoD's direct responsibility, and to avoid potentially impacting ongoing civil litigation in which KBR was involved.

We conducted this review from September 2009 through September 2010. We interviewed and collected information from representatives of the Assistant Secretary of

Exposure to Sodium Dichromate at Qarmat Ali Iraq in 2003:
Part I - Evaluation of Efforts to Identify, Contact, and Provide Access to Care for Personnel
September 17, 2010 Report No. SPO-2010-006

Defense for Health Affairs, the Assistant Secretary of the Army for Manpower and Reserve Affairs, U.S. Central Command, U.S. Army Center for Health Promotion and Preventive Medicine (CHPPM)[1], USACE, and impacted State Army National Guard (ARNG) headquarters and units. We coordinated with the Veterans Health Administration of the VA and visited State ARNG offices in January 2010. (See Appendix C for further discussion of scope and methodology.)

Background

Site Occupation and Hazard Identification. USACE was assigned the mission to restore Iraq's oil industry infrastructure (Restore Iraqi Oil – RIO) in January 2003. In March 2003, USACE awarded KBR contract DACA63-03-D-0005 to support the RIO mission. On March 20, 2003, USACE awarded Task Order 0003, covering the restoration of several hundred oil production facilities: oil wells, gas oil separation plants, and other supporting facilities, including the Qarmat Ali water treatment plant.

The Qarmat Ali facility was constructed in the 1970's by the Union of Soviet Socialist Republics, and was critical to maintenance of the Rumallah oil fields. Water drawn from the Tigris River was treated at the facility and injected under pressure into the ground to drive oil to the surface and help prevent ground subsidence. Prior to U.S. occupation of the site, the water was filtered and treated with sodium dichromate, a corrosion inhibitor, to increase the life of pipelines, pumps, and other equipment. Sodium dichromate exhibits as an orange powder and contains hexavalent chromium (chromium VI), a carcinogen. Pre-war operations and post-war vandalism resulted in sodium dichromate contamination over parts of the facility.

KBR and USACE first visited the site in late April 2003 (see Figure 1), and began regular work at the site in late May. U.S. soldiers from the Oregon and West Virginia ARNG escorted civilian employees and contractors on day trips from Kuwait to perform work at the site. A military unit from the United Kingdom provided general site security; U.S. personnel did not live at the site during repair and renovation. As shown in Figure 1, soldiers from the Indiana and South Carolina ARNG were added to the mission and eventually replaced the Oregon and West Virginia ARNG units.

According to trip reports, KBR was first made aware of sodium dichromate use at Qarmat Ali by Iraqi Southern Oil Company representatives during a meeting on June 1, 2003. However, a USACE safety manager testified that he had observed sodium dichromate on-site in April 2003, and that the "contractor was aware those chemicals were hazardous." Other USACE representatives stated they were unable to verify the timing of this April site visit, and concluded that the observations likely occurred later, probably in June 2003. A KBR site assessment report consolidating information from early July 2003 identified sodium dichromate as a corrosion inhibitor used at the Qarmat Ali facility.

---

[1] On October 1, 2009, the Army renamed CHPPM as the U.S. Army Public Health Command (Provisional). We will use "CHPPM" throughout this report.

Exposure to Sodium Dichromate at Qarmat Ali Iraq in 2003:
Part I - Evaluation of Efforts to Identify, Contact, and Provide Access to Care for Personnel
September 17, 2010 Report No. SPO-2010-006

KBR performed several clean-up actions following identification of hazardous site conditions. In June 2003, KBR reported covering "yellow stained soil" with soil from outside the water treatment plant "as an initial measure to minimize direct contact with the stained soil and prevent or minimize the airborne mobility and inhalation of the contaminated surface soil." On August 7 and 9, 2003, a representative from the KBR Environmental Group conducted a limited environmental assessment, collecting soil and air samples. KBR notified the USACE contracting office of possible contamination on August 8, 2003. Following confirmation of chromium contamination on August 12, 2003, KBR notified the USACE Administrative Contracting Officer of their intent to "immediately procure a contractor, materials, and means to encapsulate the soils in question." Remedial measures began on August 18 and continued into October 2003.

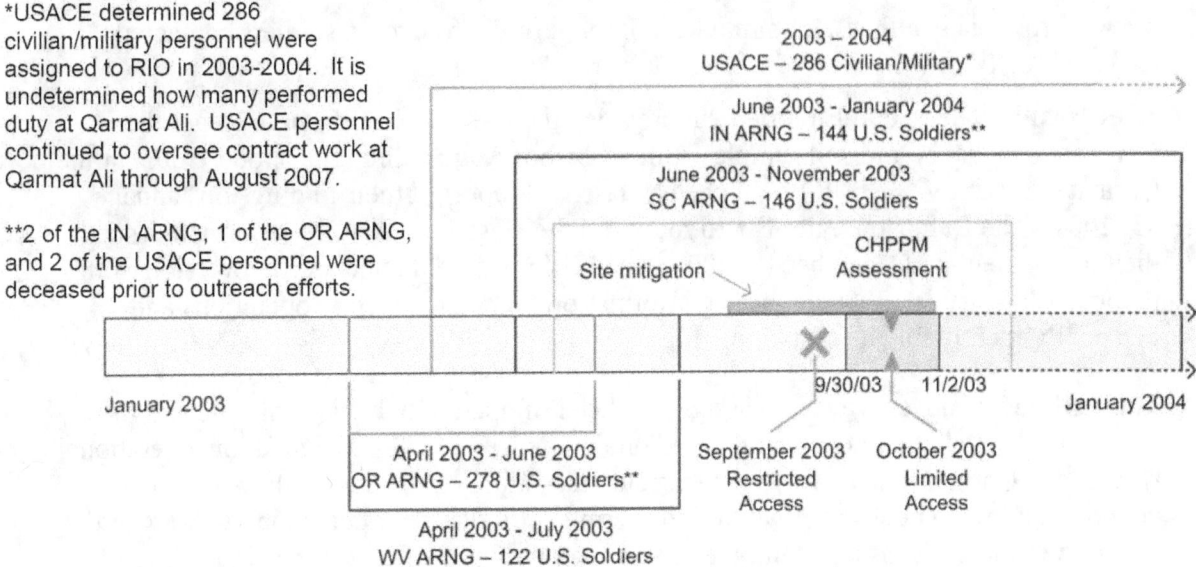

Figure 1. Timeline for Potential Sodium Dichromate Exposure at the Qarmat Ali Water Treatment Plant.

Starting on September 8, 2003, KBR limited access to the facility, and workers visiting the site were required to use personal protective equipment. The next day, the USACE Environmental Health and Safety Office recommended notification of coalition forces and testing of USACE employees who had spent time at the site. On September 19, 2003, the Combined Forces Land Component Commander issued a fragmentary order restricting all coalition soldiers from the site and discontinuing any mission to the facility without permission from the Command Surgeon.[2]

On September 15, 2003, the Combined Forces Land Component Command Surgeon's office notified CHPPM of the potential exposure. On September 26, 2003, the Surgeon sent an official request for occupational and environmental health personnel support.

---

[2] The Combined Forces Land Component Commander was the senior commander of ground forces, responsible to the Commander, Multi-National Forces – Iraq. In 2003, the Commander, V U.S. Corps was assigned as the Combined Forces Land Component Commander.

Exposure to Sodium Dichromate at Qarmat Ali Iraq in 2003:
Part I - Evaluation of Efforts to Identify, Contact, and Provide Access to Care for Personnel
September 17, 2010 Report No. SPO-2010-006

Site Assessment. In response to the Command Surgeon's request, a CHPPM Special Medical Augmentation Response Team conducted a health risk assessment at the Qarmat Ali facility from September 30 through November 2, 2003. The CHPPM health survey team performed four main tasks.

- Collected and analyzed air, soil, and surface wipe samples.

- Conducted medical screening of 129 Indiana ARNG soldiers and 10 USACE personnel who were on-site at the time of the evaluation.

- Provided questionnaires to 52 Oregon ARNG soldiers and 53 South Carolina ARNG soldiers who were still in the area of responsibility, but no longer serving at the site during the evaluation.

- Provided health risk communication to all of the foregoing soldiers contacted directly by the team or by questionnaire.

KBR Health, Safety, and Environment provided the CHPPM health survey team the results of air quality and soil samples collected from August through October 2003, at the Qarmat Ali facility. CHPPM published a classified report of their findings on January 15, 2004. The Defense Health Board reviewed the classified CHPPM report and issued their assessment on December 19, 2008. CHPPM released an unclassified version of its report on January 10, 2009, redacting information related to military operations and personally identifiable information.

The CHPPM health survey team assigned a level of operational risk to the site and rated their confidence in that conclusion based on the evidence. They assigned low operational risk for the Qarmat Ali site for "past, current, and future exposures." They further supported a low to negligible overall long-term health risk. For personnel working at the site at the time of the assessment, they had a medium level of confidence in their conclusion. However, for prior exposures, including those before soil encapsulation, they had a low level of confidence in their conclusion. The CHPPM team acknowledged the assumed data for past exposures and the impact of KBR mitigation efforts on chromium contaminated areas increased the uncertainty of exposure risk. (We discuss CHPPM conclusions further in Part II of this assessment.)

The CHPPM health survey report included 13 recommendations to the Combined Forces Land Component Command Surgeon. The first 11 recommendations outlined on-site actions for the command in 2004. Regarding identification and contact of personnel, the report recommended that the command ensure:

- "units in past potentially exposed population" receive the same risk communication as units present during the assessment; and

- "individuals identified with abnormal ancillary test results complete follow-up medical evaluation…"

On October 17, 2003, during the CHPPM assessment, the Combined Forces Land Component Commander modified the fragmentary order of September 19, 2003 and restricted coalition soldiers from entering certain portions of the Qarmat Ali facility and mandated appropriate personal protective equipment when they did so.

Exposure to Sodium Dichromate at Qarmat Ali Iraq in 2003:
Part I - Evaluation of Efforts to Identify, Contact, and Provide Access to Care for Personnel
September 17, 2010 Report No. SPO-2010-006

We will discuss actions taken by responsible organizations in response to the CHPPM report in Part II of this assessment.

Post-Assessment Actions. KBR completed work at the Qarmat Ali facility and associated pumping stations in March 2005. On November 14, 2005, the Iraqi Southern Oil Company accepted control of the site. According to USACE, another U.S. contractor, Parsons Iraq Joint Venture, provided engineering and equipment support, with Iraqi workers performing installation/construction tasks, as late as August 2007.

DoD, Joint Staff, and Army policy in effect since 2002 required active duty soldiers and reserve component soldiers called to active duty for over 30 days, who were deployed in support of contingencies, to complete a Post-Deployment Health Assessment within 5 days of redeployment. This updated a 1998 DoD policy requiring Post-Deployment Health Assessments for all active and reserve component personnel deployed for 30 or more days to a location without a permanent U.S. military treatment facility. DoD, Joint Staff, and Army policy required commands to submit completed forms to the Army Medical Surveillance Activity in Washington DC. The purpose of these assessments was to "document the general health status of...redeploying members."

Congressional Interest. During a series of congressional hearings by the Senate DPC into waste, fraud, and abuse, and other contracting issues in Iraq, KBR employees testified that they were exposed to sodium dichromate while deployed. This led the Senate DPC to hold a hearing on June 20, 2008, specifically addressing the sodium dichromate exposure in Qarmat Ali, Iraq in 2003. Two former KBR employees testified to their health problems during and after their service at the Qarmat Ali facility, and KBR actions concerning hazard identification and subsequent actions. The Chairman of the Department of Environmental Medicine, New York University School of Medicine, also testified and questioned the results of the medical testing conducted by the CHPPM health survey team in October 2003.

On June 26, 2008, Senator Byron Dorgan requested the Secretary of Defense to, "...investigate KBR's conduct in exposing U.S. troops and its own workers..." and "...review whether the troops have been properly tested, monitored and treated." The Secretary of Defense referred the request to the Army. Senator Dorgan's letter was the first in a series of inquiries to the Secretary of Defense and the Secretary of the Army from Senators regarding exposed ARNG units, and Department of the Army responses, that continued through April 2009.

On August 3, 2009, the Senate DPC conducted a hearing during which four former Army soldiers (three Guardsmen and one active duty) testified about their exposure to sodium dichromate at Qarmat Ali. The former Associate Director for Health at the Environmental Protection Agency's National Center for Environmental Assessment also testified about the health risks associated with exposure to sodium dichromate.

Following the second hearing, on August 11, 2009, seven Senators signed a letter to the DoD Inspector General, requesting a formal investigation into the exposure of U.S.

5

Exposure to Sodium Dichromate at Qarmat Ali Iraq in 2003:
Part I - Evaluation of Efforts to Identify, Contact, and Provide Access to Care for Personnel
September 17, 2010 Report No. SPO-2010-006

soldiers to sodium dichromate at the Qarmat Ali water treatment plant. We announced this review on September 11, 2009.

In a September 15, 2009 letter, the Chairman and Ranking Member of the Senate Armed Services Committee (SASC) requested that the Secretary of Defense, "evaluate the adequacy and timeliness of the Department's efforts to date, including actions undertaken jointly with the Department of Veterans Affairs," to identify, contact, and ensure access to appropriate care for soldiers who were exposed, or who potentially were exposed, to sodium dichromate at Qarmat Ali, Iraq in 2003.

The Secretary of Defense referred the request from the SASC to the Army, who in turn requested that the DoD Inspector General include the evaluation in the Inspector General's ongoing review. It was determined that we would respond to the SASC concerns in a Part I first, because the question concerned the ongoing health of effected soldiers. Part II will address the concerns raised by the Senate DPC.

Exposure to Sodium Dichromate at Qarmat Ali Iraq in 2003:
Part I - Evaluation of Efforts to Identify, Contact, and Provide Access to Care for Personnel
September 17, 2010 Report No. SPO-2010-006

Summary and Recommendations

We documented the processes the Army, State ARNG bureaus, and USACE used to identify and contact personnel who may have been exposed to sodium dichromate at the Qarmat Ali water treatment plant in 2003.

Through a comprehensive search, Army organizations identified 977[3] DoD military or civilian personnel who potentially served at Qarmat Ali from 2003 to 2004, five of whom were deceased prior to the initiation of outreach efforts. However, the absence of complete records from 2003 prevents a firm conclusion that the Army was able to identify all personnel who may have been exposed. Organizations identified below reported contacting 895 (92 percent) of the 972 potentially exposed soldiers and civilians still living.

Unit/Organization	Total Population	Deceased Prior to Outreach	Outreach Population	Individuals Contacted	Individuals Remaining	Total % Contacted
IN	144	2	142	142	0	100%
OR	278	1	277	249	28	90%
SC	146	0	146	126	20	86%
WV	122	0	122	122	0	100%
USACE	286	2	284	255	29	90%
3 ID	1	0	1	1	0	100%
Totals	977	5	972	895	77	92%

Data reported by units as of September 10, 2010.

Table 1. Summary of Individuals Contacted.

Several factors complicated locating and contacting affected individuals.

- Five years had elapsed between exposure at the site and attempts to contact individuals.

- A large percentage of the National Guard soldiers were no longer serving, and some had moved out of state.

- Organizations, especially USACE, identified personnel using conservative assumptions, meaning some individuals initially identified as potentially exposed were determined to have never had duty at the Qarmat Ali facility.

---

[3] One former active duty soldier from the 3d Infantry Division (3 ID) also testified that he was on-site at Qarmat Ali in 2003. The Army reported contacting this individual; we provide more information on his situation on page 24.

Exposure to Sodium Dichromate at Qarmat Ali Iraq in 2003:
Part I - Evaluation of Efforts to Identify, Contact, and Provide Access to Care for Personnel
September 17, 2010 Report No. SPO-2010-006

In light of these factors, the efforts to date by DoD organizations to identify and contact individuals ranged from adequate to exemplary. To help overcome some of these obstacles, organizations with less than 100 percent contact may find state Fusion Centers[4] to be an invaluable resource for obtaining current contact information. The timeliness of Army organizations to identify and contact personnel was reasonable, given that it did not recognize a need for an additional intensive search effort until 2008.

Based on our assessment, all current and former soldiers and DoD civilian employees notified of their potential exposure to sodium dichromate at the Qarmat Ali facility in 2003 had, and still have, the opportunity to access medical care.

Serving and former National Guardsmen from Indiana, Oregon, South Carolina, and West Virginia were eligible for VA care, including the Gulf War Registry and an exposure-specific medical evaluation. The VA conducted outreach with this group.

Access to exposure-specific medical evaluations for USACE military and civilian personnel is less certain. The USACE organization and mission, employing a relatively small number of military and civilian personnel across several hundred sites in Iraq, made identifying exposed individuals more difficult than for State ARNG bureaus. While USACE demonstrated their process for providing civilian employees and military personnel with medical care, we did not see any evidence of USACE specifically notifying its military personnel of their eligibility for the VA Gulf War Registry.

> *Recommendation 1:* The Commander, U.S. Army Corps of Engineers should notify all current and former military personnel whom they identified as having served at the Qarmat Ali facility in 2003 of their eligibility for the Department of Veterans Affairs Gulf War Registry and associated sodium dichromate exposure-related medical evaluation.

The Deployment Health Working Group, subordinate to the VA/DoD Joint Executive Council, reviewed and facilitated outreach related to occupational and environmental exposures, such as that experienced at Qarmat Ali, beginning in 2008. DoD and VA can use this organizational structure to improve communication and enhance opportunities for active duty military and civilians who served at the Qarmat Ali facility in 2003 to access care.

---

[4] The Department of Homeland Security through the Office of Intelligence and Analysis provided funding and personnel with operational and intelligence skills to state and local "fusion centers." The purpose of the fusion centers is to share information and intelligence within their jurisdictions as well as with the federal government. Fusion centers have access to the Homeland Security Data Network.

Exposure to Sodium Dichromate at Qarmat Ali Iraq in 2003:
Part I - Evaluation of Efforts to Identify, Contact, and Provide Access to Care for Personnel
September 17, 2010 Report No. SPO-2010-006

Recommendation 2: The Under Secretary of Defense for Personnel and Readiness, as the Co-Chair of the Department of Veterans Affairs/DoD Joint Executive Council, should:

a. publicize the eligibility of active duty personnel who served at the Qarmat Ali facility in 2003 for the Department of Veterans Affairs Gulf War Registry.

b. review policy and procedures for funding, adjudication of results, and control of medical records for active duty personnel who undergo the Department of Veterans Affairs Gulf War Registry medical evaluation.

c. develop and publicize a means to offer DoD civilians who served at Qarmat Ali in 2003 a medical exam and medical surveillance comparable to the sodium dichromate exposure-related evaluations conducted by the Department of Veterans Affairs for the Gulf War Registry.

Exposure to Sodium Dichromate at Qarmat Ali Iraq in 2003:
Part I - Evaluation of Efforts to Identify, Contact, and Provide Access to Care for Personnel
September 17, 2010 Report No. SPO-2010-006

Discussion

Identifying and Contacting Personnel Who Performed Duty at the Qarmat Ali Water Treatment Plant

The following discussion provides greater detail with respect to the SASC request. We summarize information concerning Department of the Army, affected State ARNG bureaus, USACE, and VA efforts to identify, contact, and provide access to adequate care for personnel who were exposed to sodium dichromate at Qarmat Ali, Iraq in 2003. The ability of all impacted organizations to identify and contact personnel who performed duty at Qarmat Ali in 2003 was restricted. Limiting factors and each organization's efforts are discussed below.

Department of the Army

The Secretary of the Army took three significant actions to address the identified exposure. First, in September 2008, he established a "senior level Army Review Panel, led jointly by the Assistant Secretary of the Army for Manpower and Reserve Affairs and the Assistant Secretary of the Army for Acquisition, Logistics and Technology, [to] review the issues associated with the sodium dichromate exposure at the Qarmat Ali facility."[5] The Secretary of the Army directed the panel to address policy and procedures, review actions taken to identify and follow up on exposed individuals, and examine USACE contract oversight.

In December 2008 and January 2009, Army representatives briefed the panel's findings to Senator Evan Bayh and staff members from the SASC and Senate DPC. Two panel results were relevant to this report. The panel:

- identified the units with exposed personnel: 1-152 Infantry Battalion, Indiana ARNG; 1-162 Infantry Battalion, Oregon ARNG; 133rd Military Police Company, South Carolina ARNG; C Company, 1092nd Engineer Battalion, West Virginia ARNG; and civilian employees of USACE; and,

- described specific Indiana ARNG risk communication, soldier identification, coordination with the NGB, and partnership efforts with VA concerning exposed soldiers.

As part of the review panel, the Surgeon General of the Army requested that the Defense Health Board review the 2003 CHPPM environmental health assessment. The Defense Health Board supported the CHPPM findings, stating they "…met or exceeded the standard of practice for occupational medicine in regard to the exposure assessment and medical evaluation…." The Defense Health Board also provided 14 recommendations for process improvement: seven specific to Qarmat Ali, and seven with a broader scope. We will discuss actions taken by responsible organizations in response to the CHPPM report in Part II of this assessment.

---

[5] As stated in a letter from the Secretary of the Army to Senator Evan Bayh dated September 22, 2008.

Exposure to Sodium Dichromate at Qarmat Ali Iraq in 2003:
Part I - Evaluation of Efforts to Identify, Contact, and Provide Access to Care for Personnel
September 17, 2010 Report No. SPO-2010-006

Second, representatives from Assistant Secretary of the Army for Manpower and Reserve Affairs and the NGB Chief, Preventive Medicine, visited ARNG personnel from the four impacted states:

- Indiana – From August 16-18, 2008, the representatives participated in five town hall meetings organized by Indiana ARNG. On November 6-7, 2008, the representatives were briefed by the Indiana ARNG Qarmat Ali Working Group, Transitional Assistance Advisor, and Medical Branch. They also interviewed 1-152 battalion unit leadership and other soldiers who conducted operations at Qarmat Ali in 2003.

- Oregon – From February 4-6, 2009, representatives met with the Oregon ARNG Chief of Staff, Deputy State Surgeon, Qarmat Ali project officer, and Public Affairs Officer to help develop a program for addressing soldier concerns. They also interviewed seven members from the 1-162 battalion, including the Executive Officer and senior non-commissioned officer.

- West Virginia – From March 6-9, 2009, representatives met with the West Virginia ARNG Adjutant General, Public Affairs Officer, and a representative from the Surgeon's Office to evaluate progress toward identifying and addressing concerns of effected soldiers. They attended two town hall meetings sponsored by the West Virginia ARNG. They interviewed the former Operations Officer of the 1092nd Engineer Battalion, former commander of C Company, 1092nd Engineer Battalion, and current and former soldiers of the 1092nd Engineer Battalion.

- South Carolina – From May 18-19, 2009, representatives met with the South Carolina ARNG Chief of Staff, Assistant Chief of Staff, and Deputy State Surgeon to help develop a program for addressing soldier concerns. They interviewed 11 soldiers from the 133d Military Police Company, including the Commander and three other company members.

Third, in May 2009, the Secretary of the Army directed the Commander, USACE to conduct an informal investigation using Army Regulation 15-6[6] procedures, focused on "site assessment, personnel notification, and on-site response actions undertaken by responsible government and contractor officials." Army representatives stated that the Secretary of Army was briefed on the findings of the USACE report on April 6, 2010, and subsequently directed the Army Under Secretary and the Vice Chief of Staff to develop a plan to implement report recommendations.

National Guard Bureau

The NGB made initial coordination with the four affected State ARNG bureaus between June 26, 2008, and July 17, 2008, providing background information, notice of command concerns, and initial questions. The NGB Chief, Preventive Medicine, also contacted

---

[6] Army Regulation 15-6 "establishes procedures for investigations and boards of officers not specifically authorized by any other directive." It states, "the primary function of any investigation or board of officers is to ascertain facts and to report them to the appointing authority."

Exposure to Sodium Dichromate at Qarmat Ali Iraq in 2003:
Part I - Evaluation of Efforts to Identify, Contact, and Provide Access to Care for Personnel
September 17, 2010 Report No. SPO-2010-006

CHPPM and obtained the list of exposed soldiers identified by CHPPM in their 2003 health risk assessment.

Additional guidance, information, and assistance provided by the NGB Chief, Preventive Medicine, between November 2008, and March 2009, included:

- Identifying the Indiana ARNG program as a model to follow. Communication with the Oregon, South Carolina, and West Virginia ARNG included recommendations for risk communication and key points of contact in the Indiana ARNG.

- Providing the Oregon and South Carolina ARNG a risk communication fact sheet from the Indiana ARNG, an article from the Journal of Community Health, and contact information for the CHPPM risk communication expert.

- Supplying each state's ARNG with a detailed summary of the Indiana ARNG process to identify, contact, and provide access to care for effected soldiers. In this case, one state ARNG representative reported receiving the e-mailed summary, while two stated they did not.

- Giving all four state ARNG public affairs talking points to help guide their responses.

Throughout the State ARNG bureaus' efforts to identify and contact personnel, the NGB Chief, Preventive Medicine maintained awareness of state efforts through periodic updates and assembled a central database of names. And, as described above, he accompanied the representative from the Assistant Secretary of the Army for Manpower and Reserve Affairs to ARNG units from all four impacted states.

State ARNG and USACE

The approaches taken from 2008 to 2010 by the four impacted State ARNG and USACE to address past exposure differed, but in all cases the major elements were the same.

Elements of an Adequate Response

For this report, we defined the criteria that would comprise an adequate response for organizations with personnel who performed duty at Qarmat Ali, to include five basic actions.

1. Identify personnel who performed duty at the site and were exposed to sodium dichromate.

2. Contact exposed individuals.

3. Communicate the risk and opportunities for health care.

4. Develop data collection methods to track and evaluate contact, risk communication, and individual responses and concerns.

5. Establish dedicated project oversight.

Exposure to Sodium Dichromate at Qarmat Ali Iraq in 2003:
Part I - Evaluation of Efforts to Identify, Contact, and Provide Access to Care for Personnel
September 17, 2010 Report No. SPO-2010-006

A discussion of State ARNG and USACE outreach, results, and a summary of whether their responses met these criteria follows.

Indiana ARNG

1-152 Infantry Battalion provided security to USACE civilians and KBR employees throughout the Rumallah oil fields, including Qarmat Ali, from June 2003 through January 2004. C Company of the battalion was assigned the mission, augmented by 21 soldiers from other companies of the 1-152 battalion.

Soldier Identification and Contact Methodology

The Indiana ARNG reported that the Adjutant General of Indiana was made aware of the exposure on June 20, 2008 (see Figure 2). By early July 2008, the Indiana ARNG identified 653 soldiers of the 1-152 Infantry Battalion who were assigned as personnel security in support of the USACE mission to Restore Iraqi Oil. The Indiana ARNG further determined that 144 of the 653 soldiers provided security at Qarmat Ali. The 144 exposed soldiers were identified starting with the list of those evaluated by CHPPM in Iraq in 2003. Additional names were added through a review of duty rosters, soldier interviews, and the personal knowledge of battalion leadership.

After returning from Iraq and prior to contact efforts in 2008, one soldier died from interstitial lung disease, and a second as a result of an automobile accident, leaving an exposed population of 142 individuals requiring contact. The Indiana ARNG named the 142 surviving personnel who were determined to have been on-site Group A. A soldier belonging to this group died of lung cancer in November 2009, and another died of accidental electrocution at his home in July 2010.

The remaining 511 personnel who deployed to Iraq with the 1-152 Infantry Battalion were designated Group B. See Figure 2 for a timeline of efforts to identify and contact personnel.

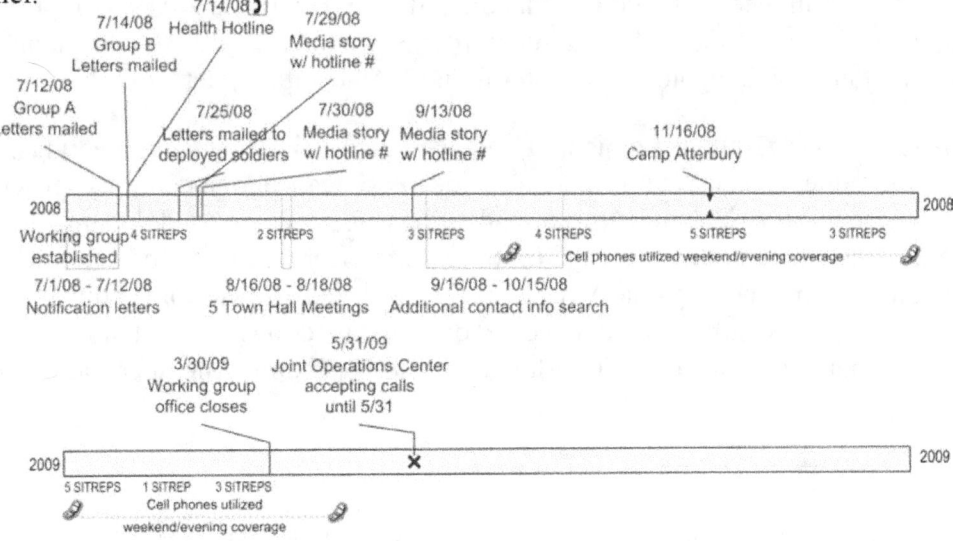

Figure 2. Timeline for Indiana ARNG Key Events in Response to Potential Sodium Dichromate Exposure at the Qarmat Ali Water Treatment Plant.

Exposure to Sodium Dichromate at Qarmat Ali Iraq in 2003:
Part I - Evaluation of Efforts to Identify, Contact, and Provide Access to Care for Personnel
September 17, 2010 Report No. SPO-2010-006

The Indiana ARNG established a Qarmat Ali Work Group in the first week of July 2008 comprised of an Officer in Charge (Lieutenant Colonel, Nurse Corps); a Non-Commissioned Officer in Charge (Sergeant First Class, medical specialist); six enlisted combat medics; and two additional personnel. Indiana's plan consisted of four key tasks:

- Ensure the accuracy of the list of exposed soldiers (Group A).

- Communicate with all soldiers who deployed to Iraq – Group A via letter and phone call, Group B by letter.

- Complete a Line of Duty determination as a permanent record that the exposure was service connected.

- Register all contacted soldiers with the VA and coordinate appropriate medical assessments and testing if needed.

The Qarmat Ali Work Group prepared to contact soldiers using data from the Standard Installation/Division Personnel Reporting System, Locator Plus web site, and unit-level rosters to confirm mailing addresses. They sent the first notices by certified mail to Group A soldiers on July 12, 2008, and Group B soldiers on July 14, 2008. On July 25, 2008, they sent a second copy to Iraq for distribution to 159 soldiers who were exposed, or who were potentially exposed, in 2003 (24 from Group A, 135 from Group B) and were redeployed thereafter on a different mission.

The letters provided background concerning exposure to sodium dichromate, contained the Web link to the June 20, 2008 Senate Democratic Policy Committee hearing, and urged Soldiers to contact a telephone hotline for more information. The letter also offered soldiers an opportunity to complete a Post-Deployment Health Reassessment,[7] obtain a Line of Duty determination, and receive a health assessment from the VA.

The Indiana ARNG operated the toll-free Health Hotline mentioned in the contact letter from July 14, 2008, through May 2009, and further publicized the number through mailings, town hall meetings, and local media articles. The Indiana ARNG reported that 314 soldiers who called the Hotline number after September 25, 2008 received an additional letter explaining how to register in the VA hospital system.

From August 16-18, 2008, the Indiana ARNG conducted five town hall meetings. The intent of these meetings was to provide facts, decrease fears and uncertainty, provide access-to-care information, and allow attendees to voice concerns and document their questions. The Qarmat Ali Working Group, senior officers from the Indiana ARNG, representatives from the Regional VA medical center, and as mentioned above, Army and NGB representatives all briefed attendees. Town hall meetings were attended by 49 active and separated Indiana ARNG soldiers, at least 115 family members, and others.

---

[7] The post deployment health reassessment was a new requirement included in DoD Instruction 6490.03, "Deployment Health," August 11, 2006. The instruction requires a post deployment health reassessment "be administered to each redeployed individual within 90 to 180 days after return to home station from a deployment that required completion of a post-deployment health assessment."

Exposure to Sodium Dichromate at Qarmat Ali Iraq in 2003:
Part I - Evaluation of Efforts to Identify, Contact, and Provide Access to Care for Personnel
September 17, 2010 Report No. SPO-2010-006

In mid-September 2008, the Indiana ARNG expanded its search for individuals with missing and incorrect addresses to include the Indiana Bureau of Motor Vehicles database, National Guard Liaison at the Army Human Resources Command, Indiana State Fusion Center, and next of kin information. Further, the NGB Manpower and Personnel Directorate provided access for a search of the Personnel Electronic Records Management System and the Defense Enrollment Eligibility Reporting System.

The Qarmat Ali Work Group met with soldiers who were deployed during initial contact efforts during demobilization processing in November 2008 to follow-up on the information they were mailed in July 2008. The Indiana ARNG disbanded the group March 30, 2009, and shut down the hotline on May 31, 2009.

Results

The Indiana ARNG reported that they achieved contact with all 142 soldiers (100 percent) in Group A by letter and phone or face-to-face, and 483 soldiers (95 percent) in Group B (173 by letter only, and 310 by both letter and telephone, e-mail, or face-to-face). Representatives stated that they discontinued efforts to contact the remaining 28 Group B individuals. There was no confirmation that any of these 28 soldiers were ever at the Qarmat Ali facility.

During our site visit in January 2010, the Indiana ARNG was unable to provide return receipts for certified letters. They explained that personnel turnover and office moves led to loss of these documents.

However, the evidence provided from interviews and other documents indicates they contacted individuals as stated. Specifically, they successfully contacted all 142 soldiers in Group A, even though 78 (55 percent) were no longer current members of the Indiana ARNG, demonstrating the thoroughness of efforts to locate exposed individuals.

Oregon ARNG

Two platoons from the 1-162 Infantry Battalion conducted missions in the area of the Basra oil fields in support of the Restore Iraqi Oil effort. Units rotated over 3 to 5 day periods throughout the area, including security missions at the Qarmat Ali facility.

Soldier Identification and Contact Methodology

The Oregon ARNG identified 278 soldiers from the 1-162 Infantry Battalion who were exposed to sodium dichromate at the Qarmat Ali facility during the months of April through June 2003. One of these soldiers died of leukemia complications in August 2005, leaving a population of 277 to contact.

The basis for the list was the 52 personnel screened by the CHPPM team in 2003. The Oregon ARNG used self- and buddy-reporting, and personal recollections of the former battalion Executive Officer and Sergeant Major to further identify exposed soldiers. Permanent deactivation of the 1-162 battalion in January 2006 complicated soldier identification and contact in 2009-2010.

Exposure to Sodium Dichromate at Qarmat Ali Iraq in 2003:
Part I - Evaluation of Efforts to Identify, Contact, and Provide Access to Care for Personnel
September 17, 2010 Report No. SPO-2010-006

The Oregon ARNG reported establishing a dedicated phone help line in January 2009 (see Figure 3). Representatives stated they used mailings (a combination of first-class, certified letter, and Federal Express), telephone calls, news articles, and a Web page on a social network site to attempt to contact identified soldiers.

The Oregon ARNG assigned a member of the National Guard as a temporary project officer from January 8, 2009, through April 11, 2009, to assist and coordinate outreach efforts. Officials stated the project officer notified 269 soldiers by first-class mail in February 2009 and helped interested soldiers contact the appropriate VA facility.

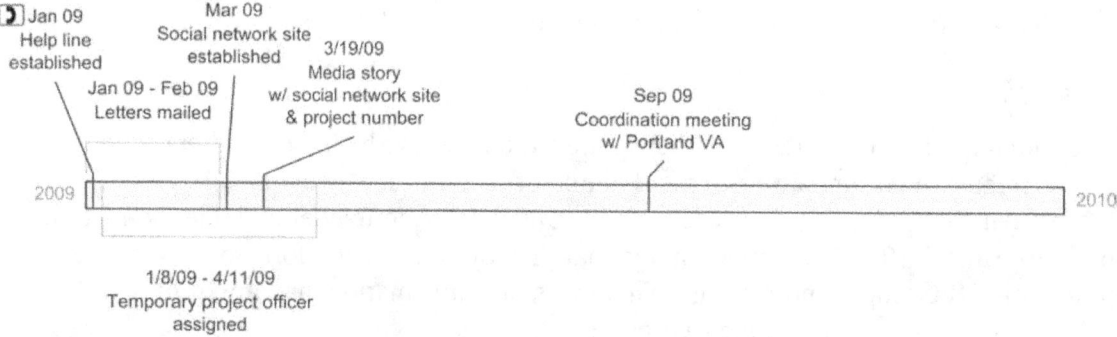

Figure 3. Timeline for Oregon ARNG Key Events in Response to Potential Sodium Dichromate Exposure at the Qarmat Ali Water Treatment Plant.

The Public Affairs Office of the Oregon ARNG established a page on a social network site in March 2009 to enhance outreach efforts. The release published in the local newspaper on March 19, 2009 included the social network site page address and a contact number for the project officer.

Results

Oregon ARNG officials stated they contacted 249 (90 percent) of 277 exposed soldiers from the 1-162 Infantry Battalion. During our site visit in January 2010, they stated that they planned to renew efforts to contact the remaining individuals and provide a briefing for all Oregon ARNG soldiers during their demobilization. As of April 2010, the Oregon ARNG continued efforts to locate the remaining 28 individuals.

We were unable to validate Oregon ARNG contact efforts because they did not retain certified letter return receipts or other documentation supporting their outreach efforts.

South Carolina ARNG

The 133rd Military Police Company deployed to Iraq from February 10, 2003, through January 28, 2004. The company provided a quick reaction force in support of the Restore Iraqi Oil mission from June 2003 through November 2003.

Soldier Identification and Contact Methodology

The South Carolina ARNG reported that 146 soldiers deployed with the 133rd Military Police Company. The NGB provided the initial list of exposed soldiers taken from the 2003 CHPPM assessment. Unit missions included convoy security to the Qarmat Ali

Exposure to Sodium Dichromate at Qarmat Ali Iraq in 2003:
Part I - Evaluation of Efforts to Identify, Contact, and Provide Access to Care for Personnel
September 17, 2010 Report No. SPO-2010-006

facility, and officials stated that some soldiers remember being at the site, while others did not. As a result, they considered all 146 soldiers as exposed to sodium dichromate.

The South Carolina ARNG established a telephone help line on November 19, 2008 (see Figure 4). 133rd Military Police Company representatives attempted to contact solders by certified letters and other mailings starting on November 21, 2008. Company representatives called soldiers they could locate and provided information on their exposure and how to contact their local VA clinic to register for care.

The South Carolina ARNG appointed a full-time Army Nurse Corps officer as special projects officer to follow up with further contact and tracking from June 1 through September 30, 2009.

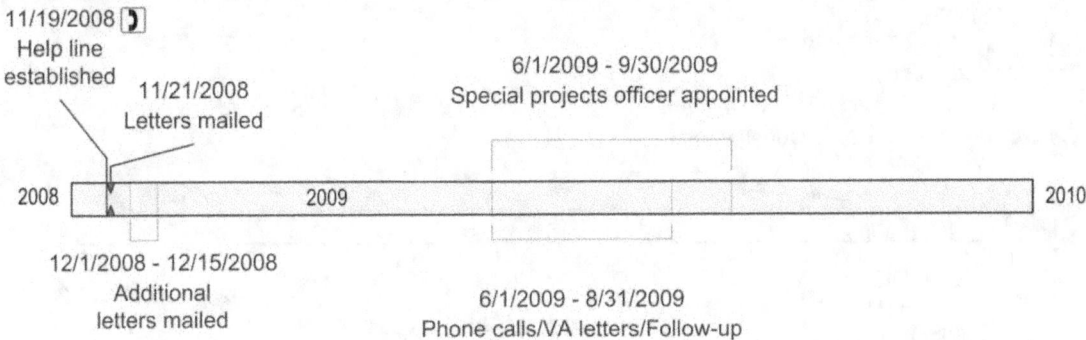

Figure 4. Timeline for South Carolina ARNG Key Events in Response to Potential Sodium Dichromate Exposure at the Qarmat Ali Water Treatment Plant.

Results

The South Carolina ARNG reported contacting 126 of the 146 (86 percent) soldiers of the 133rd Military Police Company: 64 by certified letter and phone, 44 by certified letter, and 18 by phone. They were unable to locate 20 soldiers. During our site visit, we viewed certified letter return receipts and letters that were returned unsigned.

West Virginia ARNG

C Company of the 1092nd Engineer Battalion provided security to USACE civilians and KBR employees at Qarmat Ali from April through July 2003. C Company reported using an ad hoc roster that included soldiers from across the company, sending an average of 10-12 soldiers per day to the Qarmat Ali facility.

Soldier Identification and Contact Methodology

The West Virginia ARNG was made aware in December 2008 that one of their units conducted missions at the Qarmat Ali facility in 2003. Members of Headquarters Company, 1092nd Engineer Battalion determined that 122 soldiers from C Company, 1092nd Engineer Battalion were exposed to sodium dichromate.

The West Virginia ARNG assigned the identification, notification, and tracking mission to a Lieutenant Colonel working full-time late in 2008. In February 2009, they

Exposure to Sodium Dichromate at Qarmat Ali Iraq in 2003:
Part I - Evaluation of Efforts to Identify, Contact, and Provide Access to Care for Personnel
September 17, 2010 Report No. SPO-2010-006

established a help line number for personnel, initiated a telephone call campaign, and sent out notification letters by certified mail (see Figure 5). During the phone call, West Virginia ARNG representatives explained the impacts of sodium dichromate exposure, answered questions, and encouraged soldiers to enroll with the VA.

In the next two months, they took two significant actions. On March 7 and 8, 2009, the West Virginia ARNG conducted the town hall meetings attended by 51 soldiers and family members. As discussed earlier, representatives from the Army and NGB were present at the town hall meetings and briefed attendees. In April 2009, the West Virginia ARNG mailed soldiers contacted earlier a questionnaire designed to obtain further information about exposure, assess their knowledge and concerns regarding exposure, and identify their perception of West Virginia ARNG leadership.

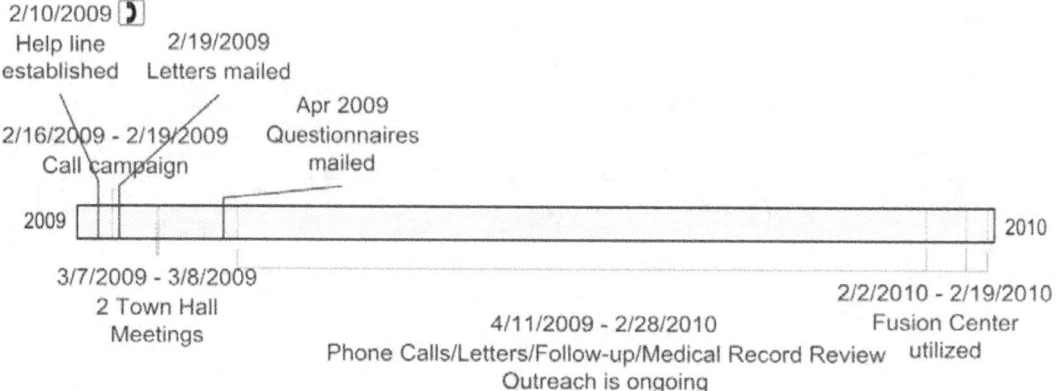

Figure 5. Timeline for West Virginia ARNG Key Events in Response to Potential Sodium Dichromate Exposure at the Qarmat Ali Water Treatment Plant.

In the succeeding months, the West Virginia ARNG reviewed medical records of exposed soldiers, focused on Post-Deployment Health Assessments. They created a standard file for each individual, tracking when the soldier was notified. The file included the signed certified letter return receipt, completed questionnaire, Post-Deployment Health Assessment form, if available, and any additional information the soldier may have provided.

During our site visit in January 2010, we informed the West Virginia ARNG of the Indiana ARNG efforts with their fusion center and contact information. The West Virginia ARNG used its fusion center to gain information resulting in successful contact of eight additional soldiers.

Results

The West Virginia ARNG reported contacting 122 of the 122 (100 percent) soldiers of C Company, 1092nd Engineer Battalion: 54 by certified letter and phone, 56 by certified letter, 8 by phone, and 4 by attendance at a town hall meeting. They successfully contacted 65 soldiers who were no longer current members of the West Virginia ARNG, demonstrating the thoroughness of efforts to locate exposed individuals.

During our site visit, we viewed case files of contacted soldiers. The files included tracking sheets, certified letter return receipts, Post-Deployment Health Assessment

Exposure to Sodium Dichromate at Qarmat Ali Iraq in 2003:
Part I - Evaluation of Efforts to Identify, Contact, and Provide Access to Care for Personnel
September 17, 2010 Report No. SPO-2010-006

forms, questionnaires, and telephone surveys where available. We verified attendance at town hall meetings from sign-in sheets.

USACE

USACE was the military organization responsible for the Restore Iraqi Oil mission. USACE reported 286 military and civilian personnel who contributed to this mission from April 2003 through August 2007.

Identification and Contact Methodology

USACE representatives were unable to determine which of the individuals deployed for the Restore Iraqi Oil mission had duty at the Qarmat Ali facility. Based on the Restore Iraqi Oil deployment database, the USACE Safety and Occupational Health Office identified 61 military and 225 civilian personnel who participated. However, they established that most of them never had duty at the Qarmat Ali facility. USACE chose to contact all individuals assigned to the Restore Iraqi Oil mission. Two of the civilians died of heart attacks in 2003 and 2006, prior to outreach efforts, leaving a contact population of 284.

USACE used e-mail as the primary method to contact individuals (see Figure 6). On November 21, 2008, the USACE Occupational Health Program Manager sent an e-mail to identified individuals who were still USACE employees. The body of the text included a request to forward the message to anyone they were aware of who was in the vicinity of Basra in 2003-2004. The e-mail included an attached fact sheet for health care providers, describing health risk information and listing points of contact for additional information. Individuals who responded to the e-mail received telephone contact from the USACE Safety and Health Office offering an appointment with a medical care provider.

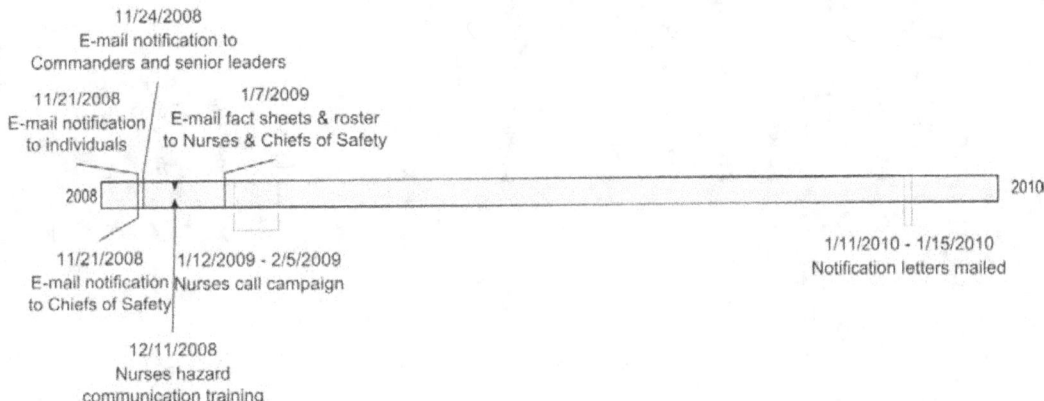

Figure 6. Timeline for USACE Key Events in Response to Potential Sodium Dichromate Exposure at the Qarmat Ali Water Treatment Plant.

On the same date, the Safety and Health Office Program Manager sent an e-mail to USACE Safety Chiefs discussing the possible exposure and describing anticipated actions. On November 24, 2009, the USACE Deputy Commanding General sent an e-mail to USACE military and civilian senior leaders, including Division, Center, and Engineer unit Commanders.

Exposure to Sodium Dichromate at Qarmat Ali Iraq in 2003:
Part I - Evaluation of Efforts to Identify, Contact, and Provide Access to Care for Personnel
September 17, 2010 Report No. SPO-2010-006

USACE nurses reached out to current employees with contact information on file, but who had not responded to the November 21, 2009 e-mail. Nurses discussed employees' concerns and provided information to the USACE Safety and Health Office. Employees were also offered the opportunity to discuss concerns with an Occupational Health provider.

In early January 2010, the USACE Occupational Health Program Manager sent letters to 35 employees no longer employed by USACE. The letter provided background, contact information for further questions, and requested individuals to forward a copy of the letter to anyone who "was in the vicinity of the Qarmat Ali Water Treatment Facility 2003-2004 that may not have been contacted...."

Results

USACE reported contact by e-mail, phone, or personal interview with 255 of 284 personnel who deployed on the Restore Iraqi Oil mission. We observed selected e-mail responses from individuals. Contact efforts we observed did not inform military personnel of their eligibility for the Gulf War Registry exam.

Summary of State ARNG and USACE Responses

As shown in Table 2, the responses to the exposure at Qarmat Ali by assessed organizations contained the necessary elements of an adequate response as defined on page 12 of this report. For this assessment, use of one sub-element in each of the five elements was sufficient, although using multiple methods generally led to better results.

Unit / Org	Identify				Contact			Communicate						Data Collection			Oversight		
	Search Tools	Roster / Unit List	Help Line	Peer to Peer	Letters	Phone Call / E-mail	Social Network	Help Line	VA Contact	Public Media	Town Hall Meeting	Survey	Call Campaign	Medical Review	Site Validation	GWR Registry	Task Force	Project Officer	Situation Reports
IN	X	X	X	X	X	X		X	X	X	X	X	X	X	X	X	X	X	X
OR		X	X	X	X	X	X	X	X	X						X		X	
SC		X	X		X	X		X	X				X		X	X		X	
WV	X	X	X	X	X	X		X	X	X	X	X	X	X	X	X		X	
USACE		X	X	X	X	X		X					X	X	X			X	

Data reported by organizations as of March 2010.

Table 2. Summary of State ARNG and USACE Responses.

Exposure to Sodium Dichromate at Qarmat Ali Iraq in 2003:
Part I - Evaluation of Efforts to Identify, Contact, and Provide Access to Care for Personnel
September 17, 2010 Report No. SPO-2010-006

The NGB coordinated with each State ARNG to identify units and exposed soldiers to create a comprehensive database of exposed soldiers. State ARNG and USACE used a variety of methods to contact and communicate with identified individuals. All units appointed a central office to lead, coordinate, and monitor efforts.

As shown on page 7 of this report, the Army identified 977 individuals who were exposed to sodium dichromate at the Qarmat Ali facility in 2003. While it is unlikely that additional personnel or units assigned duty at Qarmat Ali will be identified, the insufficiency of detailed Army and State ARNG records from 2003 does not allow for absolute assurance.

Organizations reported building lists of exposed individuals, assuming that an individual was exposed unless demonstrated otherwise. Specifically, the USACE list included all military and civilians assigned to the Restore Iraqi Oil effort, without specifying individuals who were assigned to the Qarmat Ali facility.

All organizations reported personnel turnover as an obstacle to contacting identified individuals. Officials from two State ARNGs reported a large percentage of soldiers who served in 2003 had since separated from the Guard. Significant numbers of those no longer lived in the state for which they served, and deactivation of one impacted unit further complicated efforts. Inaccurate and out-of-date personnel information created a need to utilize creative methods for locating former soldiers.

During the conduct of this project, several organizations continued attempts to contact individuals, and periodically updated their databases of information. Therefore, the number of individuals identified and contacted shown in this report may differ from prior reports. Army representatives stated that the standard was for each State ARNG bureau to contact 100 percent of deployed soldiers in the identified units and determine if the individual had duty at Qarmat Ali.

Department of Veterans Affairs

While identification, contact, and tracking of soldiers and civilians exposed at the Qarmat Ali facility was a DoD responsibility, VA coordinated and participated with the Army and NGB concerning risk communication to current and former soldiers.

VA program managers coordinated with state ARNG officials in all four states. They attended and briefed at the town hall meetings held by two State ARNG bureaus. State ARNG officials from South Carolina and Oregon reported that VA representatives also participated in soldier outreach efforts.

VA included information specific to Qarmat Ali on its web site, including a description of the occupational and environmental exposure to chromium at the facility, an explanation of potential health hazards, and an overview of potential VA benefits.

Exposure to Sodium Dichromate at Qarmat Ali Iraq in 2003:
Part I - Evaluation of Efforts to Identify, Contact, and Provide Access to Care for Personnel
September 17, 2010 Report No. SPO-2010-006

Providing Access to Care for Personnel Who Performed Duty at the Qarmat Ali Water Treatment Plant

The Department of the Army, NGB, affected State ARNG bureaus, USACE, and the VA have coordinated their efforts to provide access to care for personnel exposed to sodium dichromate at the Qarmat Ali facility.

Soldiers and government civilians performed duty at the Qarmat Ali facility in 2003. Qualification for the type of medical care provided exposed individuals depended on their status within one of three categories.

- VA Eligible – This category included two groups of soldiers. The first group consisted of members of the Active Army or National Guard who completed service and separated or retired. The second group was members of the State ARNG still serving in the National Guard. These soldiers comprised the majority of the individuals who served at the Qarmat Ali facility. They qualified for VA benefits, barring ineligibility for reasons such as discharge or release under dishonorable conditions, or not completing the full period for which they were called to active duty. In these cases, individuals have an appeal process available to them.[8]

- Active Duty Military – This category included soldiers who remain in service on active status. Identified individuals in this group performed duty for USACE. These soldiers had access to medical care through the DoD-administered military health care system, and will qualify for VA benefits when they separate from service.

- Civilians – This category consisted of individuals who served at the Qarmat Ali facility as civilian employees of DoD. These individuals generally received medical care from civilian providers.

Care for VA Eligible Individuals

In May 2009, CHPPM provided information on a series of environmental exposures in Iraq and Afghanistan to the joint DoD/VA Deployment Health Working Group. In response, VA proposed establishing a registry for veterans exposed to sodium dichromate at the Qarmat Ali facility. According to a VA official, this registry is based on the type of surveillance that the Occupational Safety and Health Administration would require for a population of industrial workers who were exposed to chromates. The official also said it could serve as a model for developing medical surveillance for exposures in Operation Iraqi Freedom and Operation Enduring Freedom. The VA reported that program costs

---

[8] VA publication "Federal Benefits for Veterans, Dependents and Survivors," 2010 edition, states, "A person who served in the active military...and who was discharged or released under conditions other than dishonorable [including retirees] may qualify for VA health care benefits. Reservists and National Guard members may also qualify for VA health care benefits if they were called to active duty (other than for training only) by a Federal order and completed the full period for which they were called or ordered to active duty."

Exposure to Sodium Dichromate at Qarmat Ali Iraq in 2003:
Part I - Evaluation of Efforts to Identify, Contact, and Provide Access to Care for Personnel
September 17, 2010 Report No. SPO-2010-006

were partially built into current funding for Gulf War Registry[9] examinations. They planned to program for funds to conduct additional required testing, with other expenses coming from existing operating funds.

In October 2009, the Secretary of Veterans Affairs wrote in response to a letter from a member of Congress:

> We are in the process of augmenting the GWR [Gulf War Registry] to reflect service at Qarmat Ali. The involved Guard members who have had an initial examination will be recalled to have a complete exposure assessment, as well as a more targeted physical examination and ancillary testing looking for indications of health outcomes that may be related to hexavalent chromium. Those who have yet to enroll in the GWR will get this targeted examination initially. They will also receive a chest radiograph and pulmonary function testing. This evaluation will be repeated periodically (every year for examination and every 5 years for chest radiograph).

Therefore, inclusion in the VA Gulf War Registry provided a mechanism for the majority of personnel exposed to sodium dichromate at Qarmat Ali to receive access to VA health care.

A VA representative stated that names of individuals who were exposed at the Qarmat Ali facility were initially obtained from State ARNG bureaus in July 2009. The reported numbers of identified and contacted individuals changed during our evaluation. A CHPPM official reported that they provided an updated list to the VA in January 2010.

As of March 2010, VA officials reported that 124 personnel from the State ARNG units identified as exposed at the Qarmat Ali facility had registered in the Gulf War Registry (69 from Indiana, 8 from Oregon, 17 from South Carolina, and 30 from West Virginia). As indicated in Table 1 on page 7, the total eligible ARNG population is 687. A West Virginia ARNG official opined that many veterans did not have, or want to use, the time and expense to travel to a VA facility for the Gulf War Registry examination.

VA representatives planned to send an information package to all VA eligible individuals who served at the Qarmat Ali facility to attempt to increase the number of registrants. The packet will include a letter signed by the Secretary of Veterans Affairs inviting individuals to participate in the medical evaluation, a fact sheet, physical exam procedures, and points of contact for VA hospitals. As of September 16, 2010, the letter was in coordination for signature by both the Secretary of Defense and the Secretary of Veterans Affairs.

USACE officials reported approximately 48 separated or retired military personnel took part in the Restore Iraqi Oil mission. VA was made aware that former USACE military personnel may have been exposed to sodium dichromate at the Qarmat Ali facility during

---

[9] The VA Persian Gulf War Registry was established by Public Law 102-585, "Persian Gulf War Veterans Health Status Act," November, 1992, to identify individuals who served as members of the Armed Forces in the Persian Gulf theater of operations during the Persian Gulf War. According to the Veterans Health Affairs Handbook 1303.02, the intent of the registry was to "identify possible diseases resulting from U.S. military personnel service in certain areas of Southwest Asia."

Exposure to Sodium Dichromate at Qarmat Ali Iraq in 2003:
Part I - Evaluation of Efforts to Identify, Contact, and Provide Access to Care for Personnel
September 17, 2010 Report No. SPO-2010-006

our evaluation. USACE provided a list of names of separated and retired military personnel to the Army and VA on June 25, 2010.

One additional group of active duty soldiers from the 3d Infantry Division was reported to have performed duty at the Qarmat Ali facility in 2003. A former soldier testified in a Congressional hearing that he and seven other members of his unit performed an infrastructure assessment of the plant in April 2003. He also testified subsequently that he had access to VA medical care. The Army has been unable to substantiate that any other soldiers from the unit were present at the facility.

Care for Active Duty Military Personnel

Personnel who performed duty at the Qarmat Ali facility in 2003 and remain on active duty have access to medical care through the DoD-administered military health care system. In addition, they are authorized to register for the Gulf War Registry and request the tailored medical evaluation.

The VA Veterans Health Administration Handbook 1303.02, June 5, 2007 states, "Active duty military personnel who served in Southwest Asia are eligible to participate in the GWR [Gulf War Registry] program." The handbook further states for Active Duty military personnel:

> (1) When active duty members of the uniformed services apply to VA facilities for a GWR examination, the Department of Defense (DoD) must authorize and provide the appropriate DoD Form 2161, Referral for Civilian Care, or equivalent form, requesting this examination, or DoD must provide services under an existing DoD-VA sharing agreement...Procedures for processing the examination are the same as those for a veteran participating in this program.
> (2) A military facility may perform the GWR examination according to VA instructions.
> (3) Military facilities may obtain the pertinent VA administrative issue and appropriate forms from the nearest VA site.
> (4) Military facilities must provide completed copies of the worksheets, physical examination, laboratory tests, etc., to the nearest VA medical center or outpatient clinic.

A representative from the office of the Assistant Secretary of Defense for Health Affairs stated that DoD had no objection to VA offering the Gulf War Registry medical evaluation to soldiers who served at the Qarmat Ali facility and remain on active duty. However, both DoD and VA officials pointed out that active duty applications for VA benefits occur infrequently. Processing evaluations from active duty soldiers would require exceptions to normal funding, record-sharing, and adjudication processes.

On April 13, 2010, USACE, through the Army, provided the VA with contact information for 13 personnel who performed duty at the Qarmat Ali facility and remained on active duty. VA intended to reach out to these soldiers and offer the Gulf War Registry medical evaluation.

Care for DoD Civilian Personnel

Civilian employees of DoD who participated in operations in Southwest Asia are not authorized to participate in the VA Gulf War Registry. There was no corresponding

Exposure to Sodium Dichromate at Qarmat Ali Iraq in 2003:
Part I - Evaluation of Efforts to Identify, Contact, and Provide Access to Care for Personnel
September 17, 2010 Report No. SPO-2010-006

process to ensure DoD civilians who were exposed to sodium dichromate received medical examinations similar to those offered to active and former soldiers.

However, USACE did offer its civilian employees the opportunity to talk with a medical care provider. In December 2009, the USACE Safety and Health Office coordinated training for USACE nurses on potential health effects from service at the Qarmat Ali facility. CHPPM and the USACE Public Affairs Office provided input to the training, which included a presentation on risk communication. The USACE Occupational Health Program Manager followed up with a fact sheet and tracking spreadsheet to USACE nurses and local Chiefs of Safety on January 7, 2009.

In general, civilian employees of DoD received care from civilian providers. However, Department of Defense Directive 1404.10, "Civilian Expeditionary Workforce", January 23, 2009, includes circumstances in which DoD civilians also could receive care in a military treatment facility.

> Deployed DoD civilian employees who were treated in theater continue to be eligible for treatment in an MTF [Military Treatment Facility] or civilian medical facility for compensable illnesses, diseases, wounds, or injuries under the Department of Labor Office of Workers' Compensation Program (DOL OWCP)...upon their return at no cost to the civilian employee. DoD civilian employees who deployed and are subsequently determined to have compensable illnesses, diseases, wounds, or injuries under the DOL OWCP programs also are eligible for treatment in an MTF or civilian sector medical facility at no cost to the civilian employee.

DoD and VA Coordination

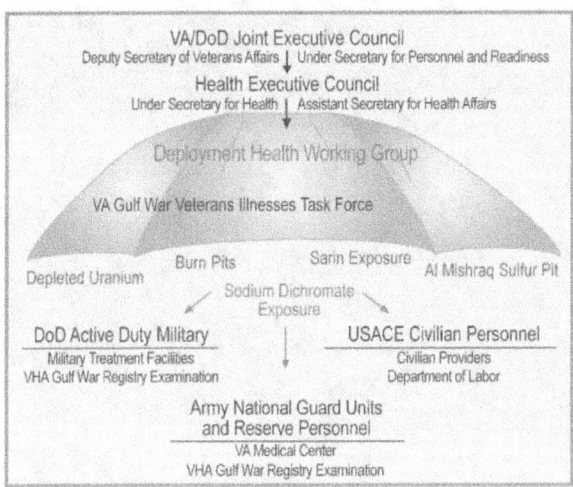

Providing access to care for personnel who may have been exposed to sodium dichromate at Qarmat Ali is complicated by the different organizations and categories of personnel involved. DoD and VA have addressed the exposure to sodium dichromate at the Qarmat Ali facility as one of several instances of occupational and environmental exposures (see Figure 7). The inter-agency Deployment Health Working Group, a subordinate group under the VA/DoD Joint Executive Council, is spearheading the effort.

Figure 7. Overview of VA/DoD Coordination for Deployed Occupational and Environmental Exposures.

Exposure to Sodium Dichromate at Qarmat Ali Iraq in 2003:
Part I - Evaluation of Efforts to Identify, Contact, and Provide Access to Care for Personnel
September 17, 2010 Report No. SPO-2010-006

Appendix A. Letter from the Senate Armed Services Committee

CARL LEVIN, MICHIGAN, CHAIRMAN

EDWARD M. KENNEDY, MASSACHUSETTS
ROBERT C. BYRD, WEST VIRGINIA
JOSEPH I. LIEBERMAN, CONNECTICUT
JACK REED, RHODE ISLAND
DANIEL K. AKAKA, HAWAII
BILL NELSON, FLORIDA
E. BENJAMIN NELSON, NEBRASKA
EVAN BAYH, INDIANA
JIM WEBB, VIRGINIA
CLAIRE McCASKILL, MISSOURI
MARK UDALL, COLORADO
KAY R. HAGAN, NORTH CAROLINA
MARK BEGICH, ALASKA
ROLAND W. BURRIS, ILLINOIS

JOHN McCAIN, ARIZONA
JAMES M. INHOFE, OKLAHOMA
JEFF SESSIONS, ALABAMA
SAXBY CHAMBLISS, GEORGIA
LINDSEY GRAHAM, SOUTH CAROLINA
JOHN THUNE, SOUTH DAKOTA
MEL MARTINEZ, FLORIDA
ROGER F. WICKER, MISSISSIPPI
RICHARD BURR, NORTH CAROLINA
DAVID VITTER, LOUISIANA
SUSAN M. COLLINS, MAINE

RICHARD D. DeBOBES, STAFF DIRECTOR
JOSEPH W. BOWAB, REPUBLICAN STAFF DIRECTOR

United States Senate
COMMITTEE ON ARMED SERVICES
WASHINGTON, DC 20510-6050

September 15, 2009

The Honorable Robert M. Gates
Secretary of Defense
1000 Defense Pentagon
Washington, DC 20301

Dear Secretary Gates:

The Committee is aware of recent testimony by military veterans attributing health concerns, including both respiratory and central nervous system symptoms, to exposure to the chemical sodium dichromate during their service at the Qarmat Ali water treatment plant in Iraq in 2003.

Committee staff received a briefing in December of 2008 on the results of the Army's Center for Health Promotion and Preventive Medicine survey of the Qarmat Ali site, which acknowledged that U.S. soldiers were exposed to a known carcinogen while on duty at the Qarmat Ali water injection facility in Iraq in 2003. The Army's review determined that the level and amount of that exposure was "well below the levels that would cause concern," and that there was "no expectation of any future adverse health outcomes for these soldiers." An external review of the Army's assessment conducted in 2008 by the Defense Health Board, which included exposure, medical risk assessment, and health communication efforts, reached a similar conclusion.

It is critical that the Department of Defense does all that is necessary to identify and contact every soldier who was or potentially was exposed to sodium dichromate to determine if those soldiers are experiencing medical problems related to that exposure, and to ensure that they have access to appropriate care for all conditions related to their military service. With that objective as our goal, we request that you evaluate the adequacy and timeliness of the Department's efforts to date, including actions undertaken jointly with the Department of Veterans Affairs. Please report to the Committee on the results of your review no later than December 31, 2009. Should you conclude that additional actions are necessary, please identify those actions and specify whether any require authorization or funding from Congress.

We raise this concern with confidence not only that you share our concerns, but that you will do all that is necessary to ensure that service members receive high quality health care that is equal to their selfless service to the nation.

Sincerely,

John McCain
Ranking Member

Carl Levin
Chairman

OSD 10604-09

Exposure to Sodium Dichromate at Qarmat Ali Iraq in 2003:
Part I - Evaluation of Efforts to Identify, Contact, and Provide Access to Care for Personnel
September 17, 2010 Report No. SPO-2010-006

Appendix B. Letter from the Senate Democratic Policy Committee

United States Senate
WASHINGTON, DC 20510

August 11, 2009

Via Facsimile: (703) 604-8310

Hon. Gordon S. Heddell
Office of the Inspector General
U.S. Department of Defense
400 Army Navy Drive
Arlington, VA 22202-4704

Dear Inspector General Heddell:

We are writing to request that you perform a formal investigation into the exposure of U.S. soldiers to sodium dichromate, a potentially deadly carcinogen, at the Qarmat Ali water injection facility in Iraq in 2003.

As you know, the Senate Democratic Policy Committee has conducted two hearings on this exposure: 1) on June 20, 2008, the Committee examined the performance of contractor KBR, which was retained by the Army under Restore Iraq Oil (RIO I) Task Order 3 to conduct an assessment of environmental conditions and operational functionality of the facility, and to make recommendations for its repair and resumption of operations; and 2) on August 3, 2009, the Committee examined the response of the Department of Defense to the exposure, including oversight conducted by the U.S. Army Corps of Engineers (USACE), testing and monitoring performed by the U.S. Army Center for Health Promotion and Preventive Medicine (USACHPPM), and a subsequent review done by the Defense Health Board (DHB).

Based on these hearings, and the investigation conducted by the Committee, we believe that the conduct and/or inaction of KBR and the Army may have caused hundreds of U.S. troops to be exposed to dangerous levels of sodium dichromate, which may have caused many of these soldiers to develop serious medical conditions related to their exposure at Qarmat Ali. We also believe that the testing, monitoring and review conducted by USACHPPM and the DHB may have been deeply flawed. During the course of your investigation, please assess the following:

1) Did the Army include provisions in Task Order 3 to specify the nature and extent of the Army's and KBR's duties to identify, prevent, report and/or remediate nuclear, biological, chemical and industrial hazards and to ensure the safety of U.S. soldiers at RIO I sites?

2) Task Order 3 states, "...it is not the intent of this contract to remediate pre-hostilities environmental contamination unless such remediation is necessary to protect the health and safety of contractor and Government personnel during ongoing restoration actions." Based on this language, should the Army have directed, and KBR performed, a timely remediation of the Qarmat Ali facility beginning in March 2003 to "protect the health and safety of contractor and Government personnel"?

OSD 09112-09

Exposure to Sodium Dichromate at Qarmat Ali Iraq in 2003:
Part I - Evaluation of Efforts to Identify, Contact, and Provide Access to Care for Personnel
September 17, 2010 Report No. SPO-2010-006

3) Task Order 3 required the Army to inform KBR that an Iraqi oil infrastructure facility was "benign" and had been cleared of all environmental hazards (including nuclear, biological, chemical and industrial hazards) before allowing KBR to enter a facility. Did the Army fail to clear sodium dichromate from the Qarmat Ali water injection facility before authorizing KBR to enter the site?

4) U.S. soldiers reported that a distinctive orange powder covered the Qarmat Ali facility and was swept into the air and onto their clothes, faces and exposed skin during frequent, intense windstorms. Many of these soldiers began experiencing symptoms consistent with exposure to sodium dichromate, including nasal perforations, "chrome holes" or ulcers on the skin, and severe nosebleeds, within days or weeks of arriving at the facility in April 2003. Given these conditions and symptoms, did the Army and KBR fail to implement timely health and safety protocols to detect industrial hazards; restrict access to the plant; and provide military-issued protective gear or Personal Protective equipment (PPE), which could have eliminated or significantly reduced the risk to U.S. military personnel?

5) USACHPPM did not begin testing soldiers at the facility until October 1, 2003, which was more than five months after the exposures began. Should USACHPPM have started testing soldiers at the site within days of when the conditions and symptoms started to be reported?

6) USACHPPM concluded that "there was not a significant inhalation exposure from Chromium VI" and "there does not appear to be any specific follow-up indicated, since there does not appear to be evidence of acute exposures." However, Herman Gibb, Ph.D, one of the country's leading experts on the health effects of sodium dichromate exposure, testified at the August 3 hearing that "the air concentration to which the Qarmat Ali soldiers were exposed could be estimated to be approximately 80 to 200 times the current OSHA limit" and "the symptoms reported by some of the soldiers who served at Qarmat Ali are consistent with significant exposure to sodium dichromate." Did USACHPPM improperly conclude that "there does not appear to be any specific follow-up indicated, since there does not appear to be evidence of acute exposures"? If so, should USACHPPM revise and re-issue its risk communications and health guidance to the soldiers who were exposed?

7) In its December 2008 report on USACHPPM's occupational and environmental health assessment at Qarmat Ali, the Defense Health Board (DHB) concluded, "Soldiers who were similarly exposed but were not studied *should be reassured that these results apply to them as well* (emphasis added)...the essentially negative results from the Indiana National Guard led to a pragmatic and reasonable decision not to extend testing and medical examination to the other Guard contingents..." Because soldiers who served during earlier periods (April to July 2003) may have been exposed to a greater risk of chromium inhalation than the soldiers tested by USACHPPM weeks after remediation, was it scientifically sound for USACHPPM to extrapolate (and for DHB to endorse the extrapolation of) test results from one group of soldiers to another group?

Exposure to Sodium Dichromate at Qarmat Ali Iraq in 2003:
Part I - Evaluation of Efforts to Identify, Contact, and Provide Access to Care for Personnel
September 17, 2010 Report No. SPO-2010-006

Thank you for your continued service and prompt attention to this matter. We look forward to receiving the results of your investigation.

Sincerely,

Byron L. Dorgan
United States Senator

Evan Bayh
United States Senator

Robert C. Byrd
United States Senator

John D. Rockefeller IV
United States Senator

Ron Wyden
United States Senator

Jeff Merkley
United States Senator

Sheldon Whitehouse
United States Senator

cc: Secretary Robert M. Gates
Secretary of Defense

Secretary William J. Lynn
Deputy Secretary of Defense

Secretary Pete Geren
Secretary of the Army

Under Secretary Ashton B. Carter
Under Secretary of Defense of
Acquisition, Technology & Logistics

Exposure to Sodium Dichromate at Qarmat Ali Iraq in 2003:
Part I - Evaluation of Efforts to Identify, Contact, and Provide Access to Care for Personnel
September 17, 2010 Report No. SPO-2010-006

Appendix C. Scope and Methodology

Our objective was to review DoD actions regarding the exposure of personnel to sodium dichromate at the Qarmat Ali water treatment plant in 2003. We conducted this evaluation from September 2009 to September 2010, in accordance with the standards established by the President's Council on Integrity and Efficiency (now the Council of the Inspectors General on Integrity and Efficiency) published in the *Quality Standards for Inspections*, January 2005. Although we only conducted a limited validation of contact information provided by State ARNG headquarters and USACE, the evidence we obtained provides a reasonable basis for our observations and conclusions in concert with our objectives.

Scope

The scope of this project includes military and civilian personnel assigned to DoD organizations performing duty at the Qarmat Ali water treatment plant, Iraq, from April 2003 through January 2004. We described Army efforts to identify, contact, and communicate risk to individuals exposed to sodium dichromate. We also discuss Army and VA efforts to ensure access to care for exposed individuals.

We did not include KBR employees or other private contractors because they were not DoD's direct responsibility, and to avoid potentially impacting ongoing civil litigation. We also did not evaluate the quality of medical care provided to any exposed individual.

Methodology

We interviewed and collected information from representatives of the Assistant Secretary of Defense for Health Affairs, the Assistant Secretary of the Army for Manpower and Reserve Affairs, U.S. Central Command, U.S. Army CHPPM, USACE, and impacted State ARNG headquarters and units. We coordinated with the Veterans Health Administration of the VA. We visited the Indiana, Oregon, South Carolina, and West Virginia ARNG offices in January 2010.

We examined statutes, policies, procedures, and management and oversight reports relevant to DoD policy and practices regarding efforts to identify and contact personnel exposed to sodium dichromate at the Qarmat Ali water treatment plant in 2003 and 2004. We reviewed coordination efforts by DoD and VA concerning access to medical care for personnel exposed to sodium dichromate at Qarmat Ali.

Use of Computer-Processed Data

We obtained summarized copies of the original databases assembled by USACE, NGB, State ARNG offices, and the VA for this report. These organizations constituted the only source for the list of impacted individuals. We judged the information to be sufficiently reliable to support the conclusions and recommendations in the report.

Exposure to Sodium Dichromate at Qarmat Ali Iraq in 2003:
Part I - Evaluation of Efforts to Identify, Contact, and Provide Access to Care for Personnel
September 17, 2010 Report No. SPO-2010-006

Appendix D. Management Comments and Our Response

We requested and received comments from nine DoD organizations and the VA. Summaries of their comments follow; complete comments are available upon request.

Office of the Under Secretary of Defense for Personnel and Readiness. The office of the Under Secretary of Defense for Personnel and Readiness provided advance comments to the draft report, which were responsive and concurred with our recommendations. Final comments were unavailable at the time of publication.

Office of the Assistant Secretary of the Army for Manpower and Reserve Affairs. The Assistant Secretary of the Army for Manpower and Reserve Affairs provided responsive comments and concurred with our recommendations. His response included technical comments from the U.S. Army Public Health Command (formerly CHPPM). We incorporated six comments into this report and disagreed with three.

- The Assistant Secretary of the Army for Manpower and Reserve Affairs wrote that "The overall report as written implies that a serious health outcome is expected in the 'exposed personnel.'"

    o IG Response: We believe the report indicates only the facts, without any implication of the likelihood of adverse health outcomes.

- We stated that "There was no process to ensure that DoD civilians who were exposed to sodium dichromate received medical examinations similar to those offered to active and former soldiers as part of the Gulf War Registry." The Assistant Secretary of the Army for Manpower and Reserve Affairs expressed concern with this sentence, stating "First, these evaluations were initiated prior to the VA program. Second, there is no clear consensus that the components of the VA program are sensitive and specific screening procedures, so it is appropriate for individual providers to determine what elements of an examination are indicated."

    o IG Response: Our intent was to highlight the difference between military and civilian portions of the exposed population. The timing of the VA program does not impact our statement. We consider the components and specific screening procedures of the VA program as elements of the quality of care and beyond the scope of this report.

- The Assistant Secretary of the Army for Manpower and Reserve Affairs wrote that "The manner of deaths [of Indiana ARNG soldiers] is not relevant or appropriate in this report and implies that these deaths are the result of the Qarmat Ali incident."

    o IG Response: The report states the fact that seven personnel of the identified population are deceased and identifies the causes of their deaths. Including the seven individuals fully accounts for the identified population, and we neither state nor imply a connection to their service at Qarmat Ali.

Exposure to Sodium Dichromate at Qarmat Ali Iraq in 2003:
Part I - Evaluation of Efforts to Identify, Contact, and Provide Access to Care for Personnel
September 17, 2010 Report No. SPO-2010-006

U.S. Army Corps of Engineers. The Deputy Commanding General for Military and International Operations concurred with Recommendation 1. His response included one technical comment that we incorporated into the report.

U.S. Central Command. The U.S. Central Command Inspector General consolidated responses from the Command Surgeon and U.S. Forces-Iraq J7 (Engineer). The thirteen comments were technical and editorial. Those we chose not to incorporate did not impact our findings, conclusions, or recommendations.

National Guard Bureau. The Army National Guard, Office of the Chief Surgeon reviewed the draft report and concurred with it as written.

State National Guard Bureaus. Representatives from the Oregon, South Carolina, and West Virginia Army National Guard concurred with their sections of the draft report as written. The representative from the Indiana Army National Guard provided two technical comments. We incorporated one comment clarifying the results of that state's efforts to contact its personnel who served at Qarmat Ali. We did not include statistics provided concerning participation in the VA Gulf War Registry exam. The report contains only VA reported Gulf War Registry exam statistics, as not all states tracked that metric.

Department of Veterans Affairs. Representatives of the Department of Veterans Affairs replied, but provided no comments in response to the draft report.

Exposure to Sodium Dichromate at Qarmat Ali Iraq in 2003:
Part I - Evaluation of Efforts to Identify, Contact, and Provide Access to Care for Personnel
September 17, 2010 Report No. SPO-2010-006

Appendix E. Distribution

Office of the Secretary of Defense
Under Secretary of Defense (Personnel and Readiness) *
   Assistant Secretary of Defense (Health Affairs) *
Principal Deputy Under Secretary of Defense (Policy)
Assistant Secretary of Defense (Legislative Affairs)

Department of the Army
Assistant Secretary of the Army (Manpower and Reserve Affairs) *
U.S. Army Corps of Engineers *
Inspector General, Department of the Army
U.S. Army Public Health Command (CHPPM) *

Department of the Navy
Naval Inspector General

Department of the Air Force
Inspector General, Department of the Air Force

National Guard Bureau
Office of the Chief Surgeon, National Guard Bureau *
Inspector General, National Guard Bureau

Joint Staff
Director, Joint Staff
Inspector General, Joint Staff

Combatant Command
Commander, U.S. Central Command
   Inspector General, U.S. Central Command *

Non-Defense Federal Organizations
Inspector General, Department of Veteran Affairs

Congressional Committees
Senate Committee on Armed Services
Senate Committee on Foreign Relations
Senate Committee on Homeland Security and Governmental Affairs
Senate Subcommittee on Defense, Committee on Appropriations
Senate Democratic Policy Committee
House Committee on Armed Services
House Committee on Foreign Affairs
House Committee on Oversight and Government Reform
House Subcommittee on Defense, Committee on Appropriations

* Denotes recipient of draft report.